D0500612

Creating Great Guest Rooms

Creating Great Guest Rooms

CAROL DONAYRE BUGG

Sterling Publishing Co., Inc. New York
A Sterling/Chapelle Book

Chapelle, Ltd.:
P.O. Box 9252, Ogden, UT 84409
(801) 621-2777 • (801) 621-2788 Fax
e-mail: chapelle@chapelleltd.com
Web site: www.chapelleltd.com

A Red Lips 4 Courage book
Red Lips 4 Courage Communications, Inc.,
Eileen Cannon Paulin, Catherine Risling, Rebecca Ittner, Jayne Cosh
8502 East Chapman Ave., 303
Orange, CA 92869
www.redlips4courage.com

Library of Congress Cataloging-in-Publication Data.

Bugg, Carol Donayre, 1937-
 Creating great guest rooms / Carol Donayre Bugg.
    p. cm.
 "A Sterling/Chapelle book."
 Includes index.
 ISBN 1-4027-1659-1
1. Guest rooms. 2. Interior decoration. I. Title.

NK2117.B4.B84 2005
747.7'9--dc22
                                                    2004025731

10 9 8 7 6 5 4 3 2 1
Published by Sterling Publishing Co., Inc.
387 Park Avenue South, New York, NY 10016
©2005 by Carol Donayre Bugg
Distributed in Canada by Sterling Publishing
c/o Canadian Manda Group, 165 Dufferin Street
Toronto, Ontario, Canada M6K 3H6
Distributed in Great Britain by Chrysalis Books Group PLC,
The Chrysalis Building,
Bramley Road, London W10 6SP, England
Distributed in Australia by Capricorn Link (Australia) Pty. Ltd.
P. O. Box 704, Windsor, NSW 2756, Australia
Printed and Bound in China
All Rights Reserved

Sterling ISBN 1-4027-1659-1

Foreword

"The ornament of one's house is the friends who grace it."

RALPH WALDO EMERSON

Whether you are a city apartment dweller, live in a townhome, or own a house in the suburbs, chances are you enjoy welcoming family and friends as overnight guests. Each situation bears its unique challenges, but a bit of planning and some creativity will result in a special place for visitors as well as a pleasurable project for you.

Since 1969, the designers at Interiors by Decorating Den have been helping clients create welcoming and hospitable guest rooms. The work of Decorating Den designers has appeared on many decorating television shows and in leading home décor magazines. In this book, these talented designers show that regardless of space constraints, budget, or style, you can have a great guest room. Every one of these rooms began as a decorating challenge that was met with creativity and teamwork. By studying what you see pictured in this book, you can find inspiration to create your own welcoming guest room.

You'll learn many tips and new ideas for making guests feel welcome and comfortable, assuring a restful visit in your home. But please remember, these are recommendations for enhancing a visit, and not intended to keep you from inviting family and friends to stay in your home until every last detail is perfect. Ultimately, it is simply being in your company that will leave your guests with the fondest of memories.

Carol Donayre Bugg

Table of Contents

8

INTRODUCTION

Welcome: Won't You Come In?

Despite Benjamin Franklin's famous line that visitors can be like fish after three days (it's not a good aroma), most of us envision a wonderful guest room getaway that entices family and friends to take time from their busy lives and come for a visit. Whether your guests are a beloved set of grandparents, an old college roommate, or a friendly out-of-town business associate, a welcoming retreat is a sight for a traveler's sore eyes.

Chances are you'll never decorate more than a few guest rooms over the years. Interior designers and professional innkeepers, on the other hand, have prepared dozens and possibly hundreds of rooms, which is why this book is filled with not only inspiration but many practical ideas and tested tips for creating the perfect guest room.

Open House

You may be fortunate enough to live in a home with a spare bedroom that can be decorated around a particular style or theme. A favorite piece of furniture or art can be the starting point for guest room décor. Another option is to look to wall coverings and borders for inspiration and color direction. Follow through with coordinating fabrics for the bed and windows. If you live in a historic town, play off the area's past for the decorating theme. Whatever the style, a room with a comfortable chair or chaise lounge will be greatly appreciated by company.

Include a luggage rack or chair specifically to hold an open suitcase or duffle bag. If your home has a separate guest room that is not used for other purposes, it should include a dresser or vanity table where guests can spread out toiletries and other items. A guest may appreciate being offered several dresser drawers to hold clothing during the visit so they don't have to keep sorting through a suitcase.

(Above) The grandeur of an elegant guest room is not intimidating when luxury fabrics are mixed with more casual cotton textiles for pillow shams and bedding trimmed with simple brush fringe. Guests can lie back on this lovely bed without a touch of guilt because pillow covers are washable.

(Opposite Page) A comfortable chair is a necessity in any guest room. Whenever possible, place chair near a window for daylight reading and provide a good lamp for the evening hours.

(Above) If space allows, a chaise lounge is a luxurious substitute for a chair and can be a perfect spot for a daytime nap.

(Above Left) An overstuffed armchair and large ottoman are excellent choices, especially if the ottoman opens to provide additional storage for pillows and blankets.

(Left) Two chairs pulled together alongside a round table create a wonderful seating area for a catch-up conversation.

Townhome Hospitality

If you live in a townhome or condo, room is at a premium. With some advance preparation you can easily transform your home office or sewing room into an inviting guest area. The most important thing to the weary traveler is a comfortable place to rest.

If your guest room has other uses, such as a home office or craft room, when there are no visitors, think carefully about how you decorate. Consider furniture or cabinets that hide a computer or sewing machine. Clever storage inside an ottoman or a table with a lift-up lid may give you the perfect place to hide paperwork or projects in progress. It's not very welcoming for a guest to have to move around your equipment, and it's sure to make them feel as if having them in your home is an afterthought.

Whether you offer a built-in daybed, sleeper sofa, or futon, prepare it with the most comfortable sheets, pillows, and blankets you can afford. If you don't have room for a table next to the bed, install a small wall shelf to hold a light, clock, or other amenities. Add a basket of current magazines, a few books, a variety of CDs, a vase of flowers, and some tasty treats to eat and drink. With all five senses nourished, your visitors will feel pampered.

They'll Thank You Notes

SITTING PRETTY

By carefully choosing a chair for the guest room you will provide a place to rest, read, or write—whatever your guest's pleasure. An armchair with down cushions and hand-tied springs is an excellent investment for guaranteed comfort. Be sure the back of the chair is high enough to support the backs and necks of tall guests. The chair should also be a comfortable height for sitting. A chair that is too low to the ground can be difficult to get out of.

(Above) If space is at a premium, install a swing-arm lamp for light and a small wall shelf to take the place of a bedside table.

11

Apartmental Approach

Apartment living has its own challenges. Limited space and privacy are typical, so use creativity and ingenuity to prepare for hosting overnight guests. Dual-duty furniture, such as a daybed that is a sofa by day and a guest bed by night, will solve small-space limitations.

Privacy may be a major issue. One attractive solution is to use a folding screen as a room divider. The screen may be light—such as bamboo—and easily moved into place when company comes to visit, or it may be a more permanent decorative element. For a portable version, consider hinging together several panels of louvered shutters. If the screen is sturdy, attach hooks and add pretty hangers to create a place to hang clothing.

Another option for privacy in a small apartment is to hang a curtain so that a corner becomes a private sleeping area. A curtain can be hung from the same curved or round rods used for shower curtains around old-style bathtubs. Look for them in home restoration catalogs or online.

SPACE-SAVING FURNITURE

Small rooms require ingenious use of space.
Consider the following:
- Armoire or shelf unit with doors
- End table or coffee table with drawers or storage baskets
- Ottoman with lift-up lid for storage
- Parson's table that doubles as desk

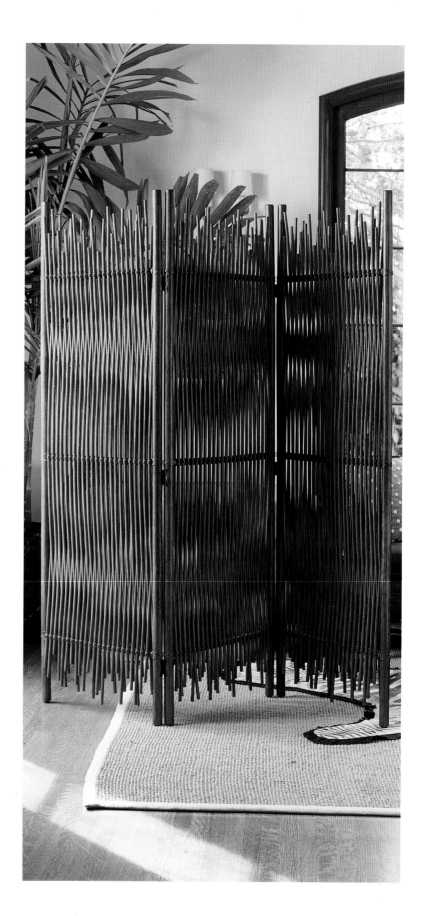

(Right) A lightweight bamboo room screen is a versatile solution to giving house guests privacy in a small living area. The screen can be used as a decorative element and incorporated into the room's décor when not in use as a room divider.

(Opposite Page) A daybed does not need to be old-fashioned—contemporary models make an attractive sofa that no one would guess becomes a bed.

CHAPTER 1

Warm & Welcomimg

Of course you want your guest room to be a place where family and friends can relax, rest well and enjoy an overnight visit in your home. How you decorate and appoint your guest room is a very personal choice. It can be an enjoyable undertaking and a confusing experience at the same time. The best way to get started is to define your style.

In this chapter we are going to take a tour of rooms that lean toward traditional décor – reminiscent of a comfortable bed-and-breakfast inn. This look incorporates antique furniture, a variety of wood and metal finishes for beds and dressers, luxurious window treatments and an array of soft furnishings and amenities.

Above all a traditional, warm style includes many decorative touches that personalize a room and make it warm. This style of guest rooms is a perfect showcase for family heirlooms and can include many of your favorite collectibles in the decorating scheme.

(Right) Amenities packaged in vintage-style bottles, natural brushes, and an antique vase filled with flowers invite a comfortable and memorable visit.

(Opposite Page) A large Victorian bed, with an ornate headboard and footboard, is the dramatic focal point of the room. The floral fabric for the bedding works well with the bed's hand-carved details. A round fabric-covered bedside table is a good choice because it does not compete with the bed and provides plenty of surface area for a lamp and accessories while still leaving plenty of room for books, a water glass, and a clock.

Color Combinations

The colors you choose to use in a guest room can make a big difference in how a room feels. Reds are powerful, blues are cool and receding, and yellows are cheerful.

Reds are best used in combination with white or a soft neutral such as ecru. When working with red, less is probably best. Red toile is a classic, traditional choice because of the amount of neutral white or beige in the pattern.

Blues are relaxing and may be used in a variety of tones and hues without overtaking a room. Soft yellows or greens make good accent colors to blue.

Not everyone shares a love of yellow, so you may want to be cautious. It makes a wonderful accent to most other primary colors, but you'll probably never choose to use it on trim or doors. Soft yellow walls can be very nice as long as fabrics and accessories offset it with other good companion colors.

Rather than jarring the senses with experimental color combinations, you will find that traditional color pairings will be comforting and welcoming.

TRADITIONAL COLOR COMBINATIONS

- Black and red
- Black and white
- Black, white, and blue
- Blue and white
- Blue and yellow
- Brown and beige
- Green and blue
- Mauve and sage
- Red and white
- Yellow and red

(Above) The only natural light in this guest room comes from a pair of doors leading to a semi-enclosed patio. Cotton sheers, mounted on swing arms, allow for either full privacy or as much unobstructed light as desired.

(Opposite Page) Red-and-white avian-themed toile is a classic accompaniment to a Country French iron daybed decorated with bird finials. The small-scale dresser and table do not overpower any other part of the room.

Meaningful Murals

Decorating your guest room is a chance to express your passions and share the things that bring you joy. You can personalize a wall with a mural or a favorite quote.

A wall mural can have deep personal meaning. A photograph of a view while on a favorite vacation or a particular point of historical interest near your home can be a wonderful inspiration. Unless you're a gifted artist, you'll want to enlist the services of a professional muralist. An interior designer can recommend the right artist for the job.

Murals can either be painted directly on a wall, or painted on artist's canvas and hung, making it possible to take it with you if you move. Consider giving the mural added dimension by mounting a frame around it. Another option is to hang a shelf to look like a windowsill at the bottom of the image.

An easy alternative to a painted mural is using a preprinted wallpaper version. Quality wallpaper manufacturers offer a wide variety of hand-screened images.

STENCIL MURALS

Many stencil companies sell kits that make it easy to create your own wall murals using a series of stencils. By following instructions, you use one stencil after another to build a multi-dimensional image. It is a good idea to purchase a large piece of foam board or poster board and practice creating the mural several times before working on the wall. The most important thing to remember is to use as little paint as possible and to keep your stencil brush clean while you are working.

(Above) A chaise with fun animal prints is a wonderful place to stretch out. A muralist vision of a secret garden is showcased through a faux stone opening in the wall.

(Opposite Page) The décor in this guest room was chosen to inspire and enchant. Deep burgundy velvet with fabrics of intricate patterns and gold threads cover the bed and drape the canopy. The pillows and bed duster are adorned with golden "jewelry" trims for accent.

19

Do not go where the path may lead,
go instead where there is no path and leave a trail.

Ralph Waldo Emerson

These Walls Talk

Wise words and whimsical sayings add a literary dimension and a personal stamp to any décor. Perhaps you have a motto you have adopted that you would love to share, or a favorite passage from a book you have read that stays with you. Any of these can be painted on the walls of a guest room.

While freehand lettering is something that few people would want to undertake, a professional artist can turn your favorite words into art. Another alternative is to use a stencil. Lettering stencils are available in most craft stores.

THE EASY WAY

There are several companies that specialize in custom-cut stencils for painting words on walls. You can find their contact information in the back of many home décor magazines. Typically you can order your wording in a variety of fonts, sizes, and shapes including curves, arches, and other configurations.

The plastic stencil is gently adhered to the wall using painter's tape or a light spray adhesive. Using a nearly dry stencil brush and special paint, the color is applied through the stencil. Once the paint is dry, the stencil is removed.

WISE WORDS

When thinking about a quote to adorn a wall, consider these wise words:

"I awoke this morning with devout thanksgiving for my friends, the old and the new."
—Ralph Waldo Emerson

"I arise in the morning torn between a desire to improve the world and a desire to enjoy the world. This makes it hard to plan the day."
—E.B. White

"Let us be grateful to people who make us happy, they are the charming gardeners who make our souls blossom."
—Marcel Proust

"Ah, how good it feels! The hand of an old friend."
—Henry Wadsworth Longfellow

"But friendship is precious, not only in the shade, but in the sunshine of life, and thanks to a benevolent arrangement the greater part of life is sunshine."
—Thomas Jefferson

"There is nothing on this earth more to be prized than true friendship."
—Saint Thomas Aquinas

"I love everything that's old: old friends, old times, old manners, old books, old wine."
—Oliver Goldsmith

(Opposite Page) Written on the wall above the window are words of wisdom from Ralph Waldo Emerson: "Do not go where the path may lead…Go instead where there is no path and leave a trail."

Classic Comfort

Fabrics, furniture, and artwork choices can come together to create a guest room grounded in the elegance of a bygone age. While the popularity of toile may rise and fall, it remains a decorating classic. Choosing different color combinations, such as yellow and black, makes a room cheerful.

Small touches, such as a monogram on a headboard, recall a golden age when families in "proper" households emblazoned their initials on most possessions. Monogrammed bed linens are available through many mail-order catalogs and can provide a similar touch.

The subject of prints or other artwork play a big part in how a room feels. An Impressionist reproduction or subjects in period clothing are good choices when trying to set an Old World tone for room décor.

THE ART OF SAVING

If a guest room may serve another use in the future, spend money on the elements that are sure to stay, such as wall paint, mouldings, and fabrics. Cut costs on items that will not carry over. For example, use a good print instead of original art to save money without sacrificing appearance. The wide variety of prints and posters available today can be beautifully showcased with a good mat in a museum-style frame. When shopping for reproductions, consider prints that have been transferred to canvas. Also, look for prints that have been treated with a varnish finish resembling brush strokes. Guests will have to look very closely to notice they are not viewing an original piece of art.

(Above) Artwork is one of the most influential ways to set the tone of a room. An attractive frame is as important as the image it frames. Take as much time selecting the frame style as you do choosing other accessories for the room.

(Opposite Page) Soft-yellow painted walls and white mouldings and trim will translate well when the guest room becomes a child's room. In the meantime, the soothing colors provide a relaxing retreat.

Fabulously Feminine

Many traditional guest rooms embrace a feminine approach because of the traditionally warm, nurturing décor. Choosing to work with a combination of up to five fabrics can work well if one color—such as rose—is strongly represented in each print. Feminine style lends itself to roses and trailing vines that can be hand painted on walls using a stencil or by an artist. The style is complemented with soft prints and stately window coverings. European antique furniture is at home in this setting.

(Above) A feminine guest room is soft and nurturing. Its key details may include a cathedral swag window covering accented with old-fashioned rosettes and tassel trim.

(Left) A female guest will appreciate a vanity chair that is lightweight and can be easily pulled up to a mirror. A simple slipcover over a folding chair works well and is easy to sew using readily available patterns.

(Opposite Page) Elegant French furniture holds court in this guest room. The bed has an unseen secret—it is as lovely unmade as it is made. The sham coverlet is reversible and the box spring is covered with a decorative fabric so that when covers are pulled back, the bed looks tailored and finished. The dust ruffles are attached to the inside of the bed frame with hook-and-loop tape and can be easily removed for washing.

Family Pride

A guest room is the perfect place for showcasing family history and heritage. Choosing a historical theme not only inspires a gathering of heirlooms and photographs, it also invites guests to learn more about you and your family. You may think you don't have anything special to feature in your décor, but think again. What collections have family members accrued? Are there garments that hold special meaning, such as a great-grandmother's wedding gown or a military uniform worn by a favorite uncle? A treasured chair or table along with family photographs can tell the story of your family's culture or adventures.

(Above) A vintage velvet coat over the back of the chair once belonged to the homeowner's mother. A vignette of family heirlooms is gathered on the night table, and, along with photographs and documents on the wall, tell a family's story.

(Opposite Page) A subdued color palette lets family treasures take center stage. A Union Officer's coat of another family member is draped over the trunk. The homeowner's monogram above the bed and the graphic letter "H" on the wall emphasize a pride in the family name.

OUT OF THE BOX

There are countless keepsakes that can make wonderful displays rather than being stored away where they cannot be enjoyed. Consider using the following in your décor:

- Baby bonnet
- Christening dress
- Graduation tassel
- Letter from an ancestor
- Military medals and honors
- Old maps of family significance
- Wedding veil

Sensible Suitability

While your guest room is likely to be used by couples, there may be times when it will welcome a sole male or female guest. In this case, you may want to consider a decorating scheme that works well for both. Most men are uncomfortable in a frilly, feminine room, while a woman may not appreciate a wall of automobile posters.

Stripes are a good neutral fabric design and can be combined with prints as long as they are not too overpowering. Prints with an animal such as birds are a good choice.

Choosing a gender-neutral color for walls does not mean they need to be relegated to taupe or beige. Consider teal green or Tuscan reds. Choose accessories and frame styles with clean, simple lines. Dispense with canopies and ruffles and opt for tailored bedding styles.

GOODBYE VENUS, HELLO MARS

Soft, feminine pillows can be quickly tucked away and replaced with more masculine ones, and are a quick way to change the undertones of guest room décor.

Feminine pillow styles can include soft textures and silk floral blossoms, beads, and sequins. For a more masculine feel, look for raw silks, leather, or suede and dark or neutral colors. Be on the lookout for a small pillow with a whimsical or witty message that suits your style.

(Above) Small accent pillows bring a splash of color or a warm welcome message to a bed. When choosing bed pillows, mix patterns and fabrics for a designer style.

(Opposite Page) To make a room welcoming to both genders, keep the colors and lines of the room simple. The focal point of this French-style guest room is a black iron daybed with a trundle that pulls out when two people stay in the room. The pair of antique prints on the wall above the bed inspired the color scheme and theme of the room. The furniture's black finish appeals to masculine color preferences and is in step with current decorating trends.

29

Not What it Seems

Sometimes a guest room needs to accommodate guests with special requirements that can provide a decorating challenge. In the case of an aging parent, a frequent guest can become a permanent one. Special needs such as a hospital bed or wheelchair do not mean a guest room can't maintain traditional and elegant décor. With a little ingenuity and the bright idea of an interior designer, one homeowner created a room that would deceive even a trained eye. A headboard upholstered in soft fabric and a hand-painted footboard along with a dust ruffle disguise the institutional aspects of a hospital bed.

Comfort should be the primary goal in choosing a sitting chair, especially one used by an elderly person. Your loved one will appreciate the chair's location next to a window that provides sweeping outdoor views and plenty of natural light for reading.

They'll Thank You Notes

SENSITIVE TO SENSITIVITIES

Many guests may be sensitive or allergic to various flowers. Provide the beauty of natural flowers without the side effects by gathering a few stems of top-quality silk flowers and arranging them in a glass vase. Craft stores sell a liquid gel that hardens into a solid resin and will fool anyone into thinking it is fresh water.

(Above) When choosing an armchair for older guests make sure it is not so deep that it will be difficult to get out of. Large, padded arms provide user support when getting up and down. An ottoman on casters is much easier to move.

(Opposite Page) When entering this guest room a visitor would never guess that the elegant head and footboard disguise a hospital bed. A television and stereo system are tucked discreetly behind doors in the hand-painted armoire.

Size Doesn't Matter

Just because a guest room is small doesn't mean that it can't be welcoming. The size of a room is not nearly as important as the details and attention to comfort and basic needs of a guest. Many warm rooms are small on size and big on charm.

Choose bright colors for a small room because dark tones make a room seem even smaller than it is. Window coverings with too much fabric tend to make a room seem smaller, so select simple styles. Shutters are a good choice for a small room because they can be adjusted to let in maximum sunlight during the day and can be easily closed for privacy.

A ceiling fan addresses the temperature control issues of a small room. Remember to choose a fan that is in proportion to your room and that blends in well. For example, if you have a white ceiling, choose a white fan.

SURPRISE STORAGE

Small rooms may be short on storage, so small space-savers are a welcome resource. Bed and bath stores sell fiberboard round tables with built-in shelves that are easy to assemble and can be covered with a standard round cloth, or you can have a custom cloth and topper made. The shelves underneath are a perfect place for guest towels and toiletry amenities. Using a glass round on top of the cloth is a good idea to protect against condensation and possible spills.

(Above) A cloth-covered round table is a traditional and classic solution for bedside convenience. Layering two cloths in coordinating fabrics achieves a designer look.

(Opposite Page) The toile wallcovering and fabric accents do not overwhelm this room thanks to the bedcover's solid yellow pique.

Novel Ideas

Just because you are ready for bed doesn't mean your guest is. Rather than a remote control, put a good book in your guest's hands. There are so many interesting classics, so when you get ready to build your library, don't forget the witty insights of Oscar Wilde or the romantic sentiments of Jane Austen.

Line your shelves with good choices, and be sure treasured hardcover books are identifiable with a nameplate at the front of the book just in case your guest wants to finish reading it at home. A self-addressed mailing label tucked between its pages will encourage a safe, speedy return.

WELL-READ CHOICES

Some all-time favorite classics worth considering:

- *The Bridge of San Luis Rey* by Thornton Wilder
- *The Call of the Wild* by Jack London
- *The Essays of E.B. White*
- *A Gift from the Sea* by Anne Morrow Lindbergh
- *Great Expectations* by Charles Dickens
- *Heidi* by Johanna Spyri
- *The House of Mirth* by Edith Wharton
- *How Proust Can Change Your Life* by Alain de Bottom
- *Howards End* by E.M. Forster
- *Jane Eyre* by Charlotte Bronte
- *Les Miserables* by Victor Hugo
- *The Little Prince* by Antoine de Saint-Exupery
- *Little Women* by Louisa May Alcott
- *The Portrait of a Lady* by Henry James
- *Romeo and Juliet* by William Shakespeare
- *The Secret Garden* by Frances Hodgson Burnett
- *The Selected Poems of T.S. Eliot*
- *Sense and Sensibility* by Jane Austen
- *Simple Abundance* by Sarah Ban Breathnach
- *The Sun Also Rises* by Ernest Hemingway
- *Wuthering Heights* by Emily Bronte

(Above) A comfortable reading area and a selection of classic books encourage a relaxing visit.

Ensuring a Restful Slumber

The finest hotels have discovered the secret to a good sleep—sumptuous bedding. Why should your guests be treated any different?

The fabric used for comforters, duvet covers, and pillow shams should be supple and soft. Stay away from fabrics that are treated with rough finishes. Many manufacturers specialize in bedding fabrics that are stain resistant, yet pleasant to the touch.

THE THREADS COUNT

What makes bed sheets soft and luxurious depends on the thread count, or, number of horizontal and vertical threads per square inch. High thread counts refer to fabrics with 300 threads or higher, and can exceed more than 1,000 threads per inch. Typical thread counts range from 80 to 700, with the most common thread count ranging from 180 to 320.

In general, the higher the thread count, the softer the fabric. With luxury, though, comes a steep price. High thread count typically is a good way to judge the quality of sheets; but remember, you won't find high thread counts in linen, flannel, or jersey sheets. Also, to make sure guests are sleeping on the softest sheets, premium cotton such as Egyptian or Pima improves the feel of the fabric.

(Left) A well-dressed bed begins with quality sheets topped with a luxurious blanket and comforter or duvet. Layers of pillows with coordinating shams make it irresistible to settle in for a long slumber.

CHAPTER 2
Gracious & Spacious

Just as small rooms have decorating challenges, large rooms come with their set of design obstacles. A guest room should feel intimate and this can be difficult to achieve in a spacious room. Take some time to look at your room on paper. Draw a floor plan, noting the dimensions of each wall. If you own furniture you want to use in the room, place it either with a pencil sketch or by making a miniature version cut from paper that you can move around on your floor plan. Start by placing furniture you own and then place pieces you would like to purchase. Place beds and bedside furniture first and then create a sitting area.

Spacious rooms can handle large-scale furniture, such as four-poster beds, tall armoires, and overstuffed chairs or loveseats. Ornate window coverings and bed canopies can work well in a large room too. Just be sure not to get too carried away and keep each piece in scale with the rest of the room.

(Right) A curvaceous chaise lounge and the metal table's sweeping feet introduce European flair to this guest room. Floor-to-ceiling draperies add to the sophistication of the room.

(Opposite Page) The grand four-poster bed is reminiscent of an Italian villa when dressed with bedding in chenille tapestry and layered with textured pillows, including an extra-long neck roll. A window seat, filled with beautifully trimmed pillows, is framed with sheer draperies on a twisted wrought-iron pole and adds to the dramatic elegance.

To the Manor Born

Guests will feel as if they have stepped into a gracious manor house with the right colors and furnishings. Faux-finished walls set a stately tone and can mimic many types of stone or textures. While some may prefer to leave faux finishing to a professional, do-it-yourselfers will find complete finish kits, including instructions, in the paint department of local home improvement centers. Trompe l'oeil—which translates to "fool the eye"—can take many forms including scenes, architectural elements, and artwork.

A bed canopy, layered bedding, and generous fabric drapery panels lend themselves to manor house style. Choosing a solid-color, high-quality fabric for the coverlet keeps the pattern from overtaking the room and makes a sophisticated statement.

They'll Thank You Notes

PILLOW TALK

If you've ever suffered from a stiff neck, chances are you slept on the wrong pillow. The solution is simple if you're at home—just grab another pillow. But what if you're an overnight guest?

Sensitivity to your guests can go a long way and can guarantee a restful slumber if you provide a choice of pillows. Pillow firmness is the key to sleeping well, so try to have on hand a variety of the following:

- **Firm pillows:** Side sleepers tend to prefer firm to extra firm pillows that ensure proper spine alignment. Firm pillows provide support to ease the stress on necks and shoulders.

- **Medium-density pillows:** Back sleepers usually prefer medium-density pillows to support their heads and prevent them from being too elevated or sinking too low.

- **Soft pillows:** Stomach sleepers typically use a soft pillow to prevent the head from being raised too high and to help keep the neck straight. Sleepers who toss and turn a lot may use a soft pillow on top of a firm one.

Even if your pillows are modest in stature, a crisp, clean pillowcase with a bit of embroidery or lace is a delightful touch.

(Left) A sophisticated trio of trompe l'oeil paintings on the wall recalls an architectural swag and old prints in museum frames. A similar look can be achieved with wallpaper cutouts.

(Opposite Page) Yellow-and-black toile mixes well with soft taupe walls and accent fabrics. Decorative piping and trims on the canopy, bed pillows, and window covering add to the richness of the room.

Big and Bold

A large room can handle bold color accents, as long as they are not overused. Choose a color such as coral or red and use it on pillows, a throw, a table scarf or the pleats and plackets of a window valance. Other good places for accent color are the welting on upholstery or trims on window coverings. Consider, too, colored lampshades and area rugs as places for accent color.

Other good color choices for bold color accents include teal, bright blue, deep yellows, and pink or mauve.

They'll Thank You Notes

BRIGHT IDEAS

Decorators agree—lighting is a critical element in every room. This is especially true in the guest room, which may be shared by people with very different nighttime routines. For this reason, it is important to provide individual light sources on each side of the bed.

While matching table lamps may look lovely, swing-arm lamps mounted next to, rather than directly over, the bed will minimize brightness for the early-to-bed sleeper and provide enough light for the night owl. If you do choose table lamps, be sure they are tall enough to offer sufficient light for reading.

Wall sconces are another fine choice for style, but unfortunately don't offer the direct light source of wall-mounted swing-arm lamps, pin lights, or track lighting.

Regardless of choice, be sure lights can be turned on and off from the bedside and if possible, equip each with dimming features.

(Above) A bold coral color used in accent pillows, a table topper, and in the folds of the window valance adds the right accent to the room's pretty décor. The use of an animal print fabric adds flair and can have even more impact when used on a traditional-style chair. The color in the pillows ties the room together.

(Opposite Page) A French-style sleigh bed is dressed in deep coral and soft white covers, matching pillows and shams, and yellow-and-red toile accents. A unique decorator touch is the small crown canopy mounted just below the ceiling.

Civilized Tropics

Sophisticated details bring a touch of refinement and British Colonial-style decorating. Using fabrics such as linens, cotton canvas for upholstery or slipcovers, and materials such as sisal for floor coverings introduce texture to the décor.

Resorting to Style

Spacious rooms can give a guest the feeling of being on vacation in your home. You can play it up with the look and feel of the Bahamas or other tropical locale. The resort look has found its way into homes not only along the coastline, but inland as well. Popular for its relaxed style with a touch of British Colonial formality, rooms in this genre appeal to visitors. Bamboo furniture and palm frond motifs found on accessories and fabrics exemplify the look. Soft sage greens mix with neutral beiges, and a sprinkling of reds and browns tie together a tropical color scheme.

Resort-style rooms are light on accessories and rely on one or two strong pieces of art to complete the look. Rich pillow trims and small wicker pieces can add a touch of sophistication.

(Opposite Top Left) Trim adds instant detail and style to pillows, bedding, and window coverings. Tassel trim, cording, and piping can be added in coordinating or contrasting colors.

(Opposite Bottom Left) A small piece of woven furniture introduces a tropical feel to any room. A small chest is a good place to put a suitcase and it can also store extra blankets and pillows.

(Opposite Top Right) Stacked suitcases create a bedside table and provide storage for small amenities. Vintage-style cases are available through many home furnishing accessory stores.

(Opposite Bottom Right) A sophisticated woven braid or trim added to a lampshade mirrors the neutral and brown tones of the tropical scheme. A decorative lamp finial is a crowning touch.

(Above) A bamboo bed frame is an open, airy choice for a resort-style room. Import stores are a good source for accessories that suit this style.

Fancy Flows Freely

A spacious room can be turned into an Old World retreat. The look of a European getaway can be achieved with a dramatic canopy, tassels, faux-finish pattern wallpaper, and a bold Jacobean print accented with at least five different fabrics on pillows. Mount a dramatic architectural element such as a fountain, plaster relief, piece of decorative iron, or a small shelf inside the canopy for a one-of-a-kind room. Just be sure to secure any heavy element into a stud or attach to wall anchors.

A canopy is also a good solution to filling a corner if you choose to position a bed at an angle. Sheers can be used for the inside of the canopy and will soften the corner of the room.

(Above) When creating a fantasy room, details count and frills are fine. Candles, tassels, ruffles, and a bed canopy work together to soften a room and make it an inviting place to rest.

(Opposite Page) A small fountain mounted on the wall inside the bed canopy is the ultimate dashing detail. The peaceful sounds of flowing water are sure to lull guests into a restful slumber.

TEA, PLEASE

Tea is a traditional beverage of welcome and a delightful way to greet guests. Knowing a few basics about tea will help you have a good selection on hand.

The basic varieties of tea are black, green, and oolong. Black teas have been fermented, green teas are unfermented, and oolong teas are semi-fermented. Consider your guest's tolerance for caffeine. Black teas have some caffeine (about half as much as coffee), while oolong teas have half as much as black, and green has one-third as much as black.

Consider flavored black teas infused with flower and fruit blossoms, such as jasmine, ginger, lemon, and almond. Earl Grey, probably the most famous flavored tea, is black tea with oil of bergamot, which gives the tea an orange-like aroma and taste. There are countless other flavors available.

Herbal teas are a caffeine-free alternative. They range in taste from flowery to tangy to spicy. Chamomile, mint, orange spice, and rosehip are some popular varieties.

Choose a Chinese or Japanese green tea for a light, refreshing tea break.

Cozy Colonial

Classic Colonial style reminiscent of a cozy Williamsburg inn can make a large room a pleasing retreat. Instead of opting for two-color toile, look for a more detailed version that incorporates many colors in its scenes and looks as if it would have hung in the Governor's Mansion. Soft blues, accented with green, teal, plum, and gold, are rich and opulent. Contrast exquisite fabrics with wood furniture and simple lines.

Colonial style is free of clutter and emphasizes the basic necessities of a room: a bed, chair, bedside table, and good lighting. Wall decoration, such as stencils or trompe l'oeil, is simple and kept to a minimum. The pineapple, the Colonial symbol of hospitality, can be represented in room accessories including lamps, finials, and pillows.

WON'T YOU COME INN?

Successful innkeepers have learned what it takes to make a guest comfortable and welcome. While you may never aspire to be an innkeeper, here are some great tips:

- Leave extra pillows and towels in room
- Offer refreshing beverage upon arrival
- Place fresh flowers in room
- Provide information on local attractions
- Put together local tour itinerary

(Right) An elegant stationary window treatment finds perfect company with this simple gold pinstripe Roman shade. The treatment uses less fabric and is much easier for guests to maneuver than a complicated drapery.

(Opposite Page) By keeping the lines of the room simple, the eye enjoys the beauty of the elegant toile print on the bed canopy, dust ruffle, table, and window covering. Gold tassel trim is a finishing touch that pulls the room together. A freehand design painted in gold tones draws the eye to the tray ceiling and the pineapple motif used on decorative elements in the room.

Down Below

Large space for a guest room may not always be in the current living area of your home. You may need to look below quarters to find ample space for a guest room. A section of a basement can be converted into a private and pleasant guest retreat. Offset the lack of large windows by using a light and cheery wall color, such as yellow. Small basement windows toward the top of a wall can seem larger by dressing them the same as a larger window. Floor-length draperies can fool the eye and lengthen the look of small windows. If you choose to use blinds or shutters be sure to use styles that will allow as much light as possible into the room.

Because a basement floor is apt to be cement, invest in a deep pad and good carpeting to help insulate the room and to make the floor more comfortable underfoot. Accent the room's décor by laying a rug over the carpet for added color.

They'll Thank You Notes

QUICK BITES

While every gracious host opens her kitchen to guests, not every guest feels comfortable helping themselves. Consider stocking up on a few light refreshments for your guest room the next time you're getting groceries, such as:

- Bottled water
- Bowl of fresh fruit
- Cookies
- Decadent chocolate
- Granola bars
- Ice bucket (or metal bowl) with assorted fruit drinks
- Non-refrigerated cheese and crackers
- Nuts

(Above) To keep a basement room from becoming too dark, choose a light color for walls, and go light on wall art and accessories.

(Opposite Page) A lace canopy on a four-poster bed keeps a room airy while exuding gracious style. A vintage wicker trunk provides storage and a place for guests to place suitcases and travel bags.

I Love View

When designing a large guest room, first determine the room's best asset. If it has windows with breathtaking views, refrain from interfering with the beauty outside. Soft, subtle colors in the room lead the eye to the beauty beyond, and are a better choice than bold tones when highlighting a view.

While shades may be a necessity, design window coverings so they can be tucked under a small valance or swag during the day. Simple swags gracefully intertwined over curtain rods can frame a window without blocking the view.

If there are natural wonders out your guest room windows, place a set of binoculars on the night table or a telescope near the window so guests can take in their surroundings. Consider a book about local birds for the birdwatcher.

They'll Thank You Notes

FAN ME

In general, you want a ceiling fan that works with your décor. To help you focus on your individual style, here are major considerations before you begin shopping:

- Blade and fan finishes that will complement décor
- Dimensions of your room
- Height of room's ceiling
- Lighting features integrated into fan
- Room's wiring

You'll want to be sure that a ceiling fan is the correct dimension for the size of your guest room. Blade span is the key. Here are some basic recommendations:

- For rooms up to 225 square feet (15' x 15') and larger, use a fan with a blade span of 50", 52", 54", or 56".
- In rooms up to 144 square feet (12' x 12'), you'll want a blade span of 42" or 44".
- Smaller rooms up to 64 square feet (8' x 8') should use a fan with a 32" blade span.

(Left) Creamy Venetian plaster walls are subtle and elegant. Applying and burnishing Venetian plaster can be quite complicated and involved. If you want the same look at less expense, look for paint finish kits designed to replicate a similar effect.

(Opposite Page) Intermingling silky fabrics around a rod to create flowing swags keeps spectacular window views open.

Too Much Exposure

Large rooms are likely to have big windows. While large windows can be great assets to a room, they can also be a problem when harsh sunlight streams in during hot summers, and heat is lost through them in cold winters. The solution is to use shades that control light, are rated for energy efficiency, and provide UV protection. Shades need not detract from the appearance of the room; they can be easily hidden under a valance or pulled aside behind a drapery when not in use.

When dealing with a strong sun exposure, be sure to choose fabrics rated for durability that are fade resistant. Remember that carpet and floors are easily damaged by sun exposure too. Keep blinds or draperies closed if areas of the floor are in direct sunlight at certain times during the day.

GREAT COVER-UPS

Utilitarian window coverings don't need to be unattractive to be practical. When faced with the extremes of hot, bright summers and cold, harsh winters, a variety of window coverings make it possible to protect a room from UV rays and conserve energy by helping control room temperature. Advancements in window shade design and materials allow full protection from the sun without sacrificing daylight. Choose window shades and privacy sheers with

complementary fabrics. By pairing similarly styled, colored, and textured fabrics, you can easily mix and match horizontal and vertical window coverings that provide optimum protection.

(Left) Large windows with harsh sun exposure can be covered with shades to diffuse light into the room and protect furniture and fabrics from damaging UV rays.

(Opposite Page) The headboard of a large "President's Bed" is upholstered in heavy sage green velveteen. This stately fabric is very durable and is used for the dust ruffle and to cover a storage ottoman.

CHAPTER 3
Down-Home Style

To say a room is homey is a broad statement, yet homes have nearly as many definitions as there are people who live in them. A guest room can be decked out in full Americana, channel a seaside cottage, or simply incorporate collectibles and heirlooms. A room with down-home decorating evokes the warmth and security of a happy homecoming to grandmother's house after having been away for years. It is not trendy or hip; rather it's a classic year-in and year-out style.

A guest room done in down-home style may use an heirloom quilt as a focal point. A hand-knitted or crochet blanket might be used as a cozy accessory. Lace or cutwork doilies may be used to adorn and protect a dresser.

Just don't sacrifice form for function. If a small antique rocker looks wonderful in the room, but is uncomfortable, just use it for decoration and provide another chair for sitting.

You'll know down-home style when you see it. It's what makes you comfortable.

(Right) When accessorizing a room for "down-home" appeal, replace high-tech electronics on the bedside with a vintage-style clock and antique lamp.

(Opposite Page) Overnight guests are treated to a room of precious heirlooms, family antiques, and a soft bed covered with a pretty quilt. A romantic hope chest and an early 1900s knitting chair add to a relaxed, comfortable feeling.

Hidden Treasures

Surrounded by our possessions every day, sometimes we fail to realize what treasures we have. One special piece of inherited furniture such as a dresser or bureau can inspire an entire room design. The secret to home-style decorating is using heirlooms and family photos and accessories that may have been tucked away for safekeeping and forgotten. A good look through closets and storage areas may turn up some great finds. Also, relatives may have pieces they would be happy to share rather than hiding them in storage.

When shopping for new furniture, look for pieces that don't compete with your antiques. An iron or brass bed is a good match with vintage wood pieces.

(Above) When one 12-year-old outgrew her playroom, her mother seized the opportunity to decorate a room that would serve as both a cozy place for adult guests and a space to accommodate her daughter's sleepovers.

(Left) Crochet pillow shams are reminiscent of a grandmother's house in years gone by. Pay tribute to the former owner of a treasured antique piece by displaying his or her photo in a frame nearby.

(Opposite Page) A trundle daybed in an antique brass finish makes an attractive complement to the inherited antique dresser. The walls are soft white to keep the room from becoming overpowering.

Beach Cottage Comfort

The cozy feel of a seaside cottage will immediately evoke deep relaxation. Whether a guest room is indeed at the ocean's edge or miles from water, it can become its own breezy, summery space.

Weather-beaten furniture finishes, a shutter reused as a headboard, and an oar hung as a drapery rod are a few ways to pull the look together. Blue and white are natural choices for a beach color scheme, especially because blue is known for its calming effect.

Salvage pieces such as an old window work well with the décor in a beach cottage room. Rough-hewn boards can be installed or walls can be faux painted to add texture and authenticity to the seaside décor. Shells, nautical antiques, and treasures collected from beachcombing outings make perfect accessories.

(Above) Walls faux painted to look like weathered boards and a salvaged window launch the seaside theme of this guest room. A canvas deck chair is an inexpensive seating solution.

(Left) Vintage wood spools make unique candle holders and bring a vintage touch to the décor.

(Opposite Page) A white headboard in a shutter pattern and a Cape May chest are perfect furniture choices for a seaside room. Drapery panels are hung by boat rope strung through brass grommets. The drapery rod is left unfinished; the hardware was sprayed gold to resemble the brass fittings on a boat.

1966
Spring Dress Parade
U.S. Naval Academy

Ship Shape

A nautical guest room is an ageless, gender-pleasing style. Side step the typical red, white, and blue color scheme and achieve an offshore feeling with greens and khaki tones with accessories that beam the nautical message.

Stripes and plaids go together when used within the same color palette. A khaki stripe works well on walls, and can be joined by a plaid that features the same khaki tone along with other complementary colors.

Often a bedroom evolves into a guest room when a grown child leaves home. Don't put guests in a shrine of soccer trophies and report cards; rather, thin out memorabilia, leaving only the most interesting items as part of the décor. Take a critical look at a room that may be in need of a makeover to achieve a great guest room.

When converting a child's room to a guest room, take a close look at the condition of the bedding, pillow shams, window coverings, and other soft furnishings that have been in use for some time. If they are beyond the benefit of a good cleaning, replace them. Also, turn a critical eye to the color scheme of the room. While the condition of the paint may still look acceptable, the colors may evoke the same emotion as harvest gold kitchen appliances—it's time to update.

(Above) A nautical theme can be achieved in colors other than the predictable red, white, and blue. Soft khaki and green are a more subtle choice. The pictures and insignias in this room are from a son's days at the U.S. Naval Academy in Annapolis, which would be of interest to any guest.

(Opposite Page) Don't be tempted to start calling a child's former bedroom a guest room. Redecorate as needed and minimize childhood mementos, leaving only a small, loving collection.

A Whimsical Welcome

Injecting a sense of humor into a guest room makes it appeal to guests of all ages. A neutral color palette such as beige and gray work for all age groups. Whimsical accessories will bring smiles to visitors young and old. A fun bedside lamp, area rug, and small tabletop accessories help ignite an adventurous or light-hearted spirit.

Put vintage board games or classics like chess and checkers in the room for quiet hours. What a happy memory a child could have of learning to play chess while a guest in your home! A deck of cards is fun too.

They'll Thank You Notes

GREAT GAMES

A few classic board games tucked away in a guest room lend a whimsical touch and invite guests to take time for some fun while visiting. A few you might consider are:

- Checkers
- Chutes and Ladders
- Monopoly
- Scrabble
- Sorry
- Yahtzee

(Right) The classic game of chess takes on a sense of safari adventure with hand-carved pieces that match the theme of the room.

(Opposite Page) Walls painted a khaki color are a classic contrast to white mouldings. Using neutral colors for walls and fabrics makes it easy to change the theme by replacing the less expensive accessories.

Popular Destination

If you are fortunate enough to live in a resort area, there is no doubt you will have plenty of house guests. Your guest room décor can reflect the highlights of the local area. Lighthouse nearby? Are there local crafters such as quilters, or perhaps a railroad museum or golf course, in the area? Any of these are great inspirations for a guest room. If you live near the water, your guest room can have a beach or boating motif. Choose a theme you enjoy that will let you use some of the things you treasure. Look for fabrics with small prints of sailor knots, stars, shells, or fish.

They'll Thank You Notes

AT THEIR SERVICE

If you live by popular attractions and tourist locales, consider preparing a basket with the following useful information:

- Guide books
- Historical books
- Local newspapers
- Maps
- Regional magazines
- Theme park brochures and discount coupons
- Tour brochures that include hours of operation and admission information

If you live near water, include:

- Beach chairs
- Beach towels
- Sun hat
- Sunscreen

(Above) A guest room has a warm, homey feel if the theme is not overpowering. Simple touches such as a small print of sailor knots on fabric window coverings or an oar propped in a corner convey a waterside theme without overtaking the room.

(Opposite Page) A comfortable "down-home" room lends itself to lovely mis-matched furniture. Small touches of a bright color on items such as a lampshade, pillows, and fresh flowers give the room a bright spark.

Three Cheers, You're Here!

There will be no mistaking where loyalties lie when you choose the down-home style of patriotic red, white, and blue. This is one decorating scheme in which bold is better. Stars and stripes mix well with other graphic shapes in a flourish of color.

Using a bold patterned wallpaper part way up the wall to chair-rail height then topping off the wall with a more neutral paper or paint color keeps the room from becoming too busy. A focal point is important in such a boldly decorated room. A large, vintage quilt hung on a wall draws instant attention and adds to the Americana theme. Simple Colonial furniture is a good choice because it does not compete with graphic elements in other parts of a room's décor.

HONOR OLD GLORY

Stars and stripes are a popular decorating motif. Out of respect for the flag of the United States of America, we observe a code of etiquette for its use. When decorating, be sure not to use an actual flag for any purpose other than respectfully hanging it on a wall. According to the Code of Respect:

The flag should not be used as a drapery, or for covering a speaker's desk, draping a platform, or for any decoration in general. Bunting of blue, white, and red stripes is available for these purposes. The blue stripe of the bunting should be on the top.

The flag should not be embroidered, printed, or otherwise impressed on such articles as cushions, handkerchiefs, napkins, boxes, or anything intended to be discarded after temporary use.

The flag should never have placed on it, or attached to it, any mark, insignia, letter, word, number, figure, or drawing of any kind.

The flag should never be used as a receptacle for receiving, holding, carrying, or delivering anything.

When displaying the flag against a wall, vertically or horizontally, the flag's union stars should be at the top, to the flag's own right, and to the observer's left.

(Left) A collection of folk art is right at home in a patriotic guest room. Look for accessories made with traditional handcrafted arts such as quilting and tole painting to carry out the theme.

(Opposite Page) A vintage Americana quilt hung on the wall is the perfect focal point in a room and is bold testimony to national pride. Quilt hangers can be purchased in a variety of sizes.

Under the Eaves

With a creative approach, the most out-of-the-way space can become a wonderful hideaway. Consider turning unused attic space into a guest room. Open beams and rafters can be masked by covering them with plywood or sheetrock and upholstering the surface with inexpensive ticking. The result can be a cozy cocoon-like room that is soft and warm.

Celebrate the beauty of simplicity with an open closet and just enough furniture to make the room comfortable. Simple sewing projects such as a shoe bag and padded hangers add a warm touch to the room.

(Above) A wooden settee is softened with a seat cushion and pillows and provides an inviting place to sit. Casual fabrics that can be easily washed are comfortable and low maintenance.

(Right) A simple, open closet is in keeping with the casual, relaxed feel of this attic hideaway.

(Opposite Page) Choosing just one fabric in a small room creates a warm, cozy feeling. The bed in an attic room can be pushed under the eaves during the day and pulled out from the wall for sleeping to avoid bumped heads.

CHAPTER 4
No Frills

You may shiver at the thought of flea-market finds or ultra-feminine décor, preferring a sleeker decorating approach. A luxurious ensemble of a reversible comforter, tailored bed skirt, multiple shams, and decorative pillows need not be superfluous. Luxury can abound in a no-frills setting with an understated approach and a warm color palette.

Truly the best guide for decorating a guest room is to create a room that you would like to stay in yourself. You may want to make the bed the focal point, and dispense with too many accessories and trimmings.

If you can, provide simple luxuries. When people are out of their usual routine, they generally have time to do some of the things they yearn for, such as catching up on letter writing. Some nice note paper and envelopes from your own stash and a few stamps would be greatly appreciated.

They'll Thank You Notes

THE WRITE STUFF

If your guests are visiting from afar, surely they're eager to share their good times with a friend or family member. So why not make the task of tourist easier? With a few elements tucked inside a desk or basket, guests will be inspired to take up the lost art of letter writing. Some items to have available:

- Address book that includes mutual friends and family
- Calendar or clock with date
- Copy of *"Art of Letter Writing"* by Lassor Blumenthal
- Envelopes
- Fountain pen (black)
- Notecards
- Postcards (from your town and local sights)
- Stamps
- Stationery

(Above) An ensemble of stationery is a thoughtful addition for visiting guests who may want to spend leisure time catching up on correspondence. If there is not a sufficient writing surface in the room, include a lap desk.

(Opposite Page) A rich "coffee shop" palette and a well-appointed bed make this simple room a luxurious retreat. A minimalist approach should still provide a place to sit and write in addition to a place to sleep.

71

Monochromatic Schemes

A monochromatic color scheme can be soothing and keeps a room from feeling overdone. It is not necessary that everything in the room be the same color, just that tones and hues blend well. For instance, bedding and draperies in soft plum tones blend well with light gray walls and pewter-finish metal furniture.

Carpeting and area rugs should be a part of the monochromatic scheme too. They should blend well with the rest of the room. Use small amounts of contrasting color in accessories such as silk floral arrangements.

(Above) Metal furniture in a soft pewter finish and with whimsical lines makes a guest room a happy place. Choosing monochromatic tones for walls and carpet allows the purple used in the bedcovering to become a dramatic focal point in the room.

(Left) A dressing table is a luxury that is sure to please. A large mirror with good lighting nearby makes dressing a pleasure.

(Opposite Page) Choosing soft purple for accent pillows rather than for the comforter ensures that purple does not overpower the room. The stripes in the wallpaper and bed skirt gently tie the décor together.

Peace Be With You

The tranquility of Chinese-inspired décor introduces a sense of calm and relaxation in a guest room. Soft, golden walls and carpet quietly complement the stimulating reds and blacks of traditional Asian style. Incorporate matchstick shades for windows, bamboo and black lacquer furniture, and calligraphy of meaningful symbols, into the setting.

Each element of the room should be simple. Artwork showcased thoughtfully will be enjoyed for its graceful simplicity. Tailored lines for bedding and soft furnishings are appropriate in Oriental décor.

Up-lighting a small tree or large plant provides a soft but dramatic touch to the room. You may wish to provide incense or a scented candle to awaken the senses.

(Above) A panel made from the same sheer fabric used on the windows outlined with an Asian-inspired fabric provides a simple and elegant background for displaying antique woodcarvings.

(Left) A bamboo worship altar makes an interesting accessory when set on an Oriental chest. Using a small floor light to illuminate a bamboo tree softens the corner of the room.

(Opposite Page) Bedding should be kept simple in detail in an Asian-inspired room. The dramatic colors of the silk fabric and carefully chosen tassels come together to create a textural collage.

Tourist Trade

Generally, overnight guests have traveled some distance to be with you. A guest room is the perfect place to share your own travel adventures, especially if you display images from trips shared with the same guests. However, it will only work in a no-frills room if the pictures and collectibles are well organized and showcased in a professional frame.

Today's framing techniques can turn just about any piece of travel memorabilia into a work of wall art. Consider framing unusual artifacts such as tribal jewelry, a collectible knife, or foreign money. These can be creatively matted and displayed in a memory box to preserve and showcase for many years to come.

Neutral tones on walls and fabrics allow the display of an eclectic mix of keepsakes. Camels, browns, and grays work well in a travel-inspired room. Just remember the three "S"s—a place to sleep, sit, and see.

(Above) A professional framer can take an eclectic array of artifacts and travel memorabilia, mount them in a shadow box, and create an interesting focal point for an adventure-inspired guest room.

(Left) Tones of brown and black mix with framed artwork and memorabilia gathered on travels around the world.

(Opposite Page) Professional framing is important because it creates attractive wall art and preserves valuable collectibles and photographs. When hanging a wall collage of frames, lay the pieces on the floor and trace a paper template of each element. Experiment by placing these templates on the wall for placement before hanging the frames.

Clean Lines

A contemporary bedroom with a clean, uncluttered feel can be soft and welcoming. Supple velvets and shimmering sheers bring an ethereal element to a room. Pewter-finish metal furniture with clean lines ensures that the room has an open feel. Bold wall color—such as purple—creates a sense of drama.

Paint seems to appear darker once it has dried, so be sure to test several shades on small areas of the wall before painting the whole room. If you do find the room is too dark after paint has been applied, try going over the walls with a light paint wash. Mix two parts white paint to five parts water and apply it with a sea sponge in circular motions.

(Above) Keep accessories to a minimum in a contemporary room. Fresh flowers are always a welcome touch and add instant color.

(Left) A simple window treatment takes an imaginative twist with diamond-shaped finials and drapery hooks and a soft rope garland hung from a rod.

(Opposite Page) Contemporary style can be warm and welcoming when the color palette and fabric texture is soft. Small splashes of pink introduce a bit of drama.

Suite Dreams

A good mattress can be the difference between a good night's sleep and a nightmare of tossing and turning. The greatest gift you can give your guest is a quality mattress.

Yet when it comes to choosing a mattress for your guest room, how do you decide? Some sleepers prefer a firm mattress, which may cause others a sleepless night.

While you can't make a soft mattress firm, you can soften a firm mattress by layering one of the following:

- Air-filled mattress topper
- Down-filled topper
- Featherbed
- Memory foam bed
- Memory foam mattress topper

Invest in a quality mattress that is stable and supportive and you'll be repaid with well-rested friends and family.

They'll Thank You Notes

BEST BETS FOR REST

Here's what to look for when buying a mattress for a guest room:

- **Coil Count:** The density of coils is most important, not necessarily the shape. The coil count is measured by how many of that particular coil would be used in a full-size mattress. The more the better.

- **Comfort:** This may seem obvious, but don't overlook it. Lie down for at least 5 or 10 minutes, and really concentrate on how the mattress feels.

- **Support:** What you want is a mattress that allows pressure points, such as heels, buttocks, and shoulders, to slightly sink into the surface so the rest of the body is supported as well.

Lying in the bed should be only part of the decision. Today's mattresses are much deeper than a decade ago. Be sure it's easy to get in and out of the bed.

(Above) Many frames are available with headboards only.

(Top) A beautiful bed will be truly appreciated if it includes a good mattress. Take time to lie down and check for comfort.

(Opposite Page) An iron bed can be ornate, or simple, depending on your taste. A wide variety of finishes makes it possible to customize the bed to a color scheme.

Iron-Clad Style

While all of the details you put into making a guest room special are important, nothing is more important than the bed you choose. The next most important consideration after the mattress is the bed frame. The options are endless, and one of the most decorative choices is an iron bed. These metal beds were a staple of Victorian décor, but fell out of favor in the 1940s when World War II created a demand for iron. Graceful design lines and a growing variety of finishes have made iron beds a popular choice once again.

When shopping for an iron bed, pay close attention to the construction. Look for solid forged handcrafted quality. The bed should be made from heavy gauge iron, and each piece should be welded together. All welded areas should be smooth and not visible. Decorative castings should be hand poured directly over the welded iron to create a solid one-piece bed. The finish should be powder coated, electrostatically applied, and baked in specialty ovens at extremely high temperatures to ensure durability.

(Right) A high-end leather sofa pulls out to reveal its dual purpose. When choosing a pullout sofa, be very discerning when checking mattresses. There is no need to sacrifice sleeping comfort; sofa beds are available with top-quality mattresses.

(Opposite Page) A sleek, leather daybed, horizontal stripes on walls, and matching draperies effectively broaden the width of this narrow room.

Leather Bound

The sleek look of leather furniture is attractive for its durability and clean lines. If a guest room calls for a masculine look, a leather bed may be the right choice.

A contemporary leather-bound daybed can serve as comfortable seating by day and a relaxing place to sleep at night. Dress the daybed with a tailored mattress cover and simple throw pillows so it is well disguised as a couch. Another option is a leather sofa that will surprise guests when it pulls out into a bed.

Leather lends itself to pared-down style that includes geometric shapes, blocks of color, and stripes in accompanying furnishings. Because leather furniture tends to have a heavy look, mixing it with pieces made with lighter materials—such as bamboo—will keep the room in proportion and allow the leather piece be a focal point.

When purchasing leather furniture be sure that it is constructed of quality hides and properly dyed.

CHAPTER 5
Separate Beds

The days of Ozzie and Harriett slipping into matching twin beds are long gone, but the practicality of separate beds is not. Twin beds can accommodate a variety of guest combinations. A mother and child, a grandchild and childhood friend, or a pair of girlfriends will appreciate separate beds.

There are many design options with twin beds. They can be permanent, cozy built-ins, or arranged to be easily pushed together to make a king-size bed for visiting couples. Another advantage of twin beds is that they allow for several different furniture arrangements in a room, making it easy to rearrange when you are in the mood for change.

Twin beds can be a bit confining for tall or larger adults, so consider extra-long twins available from most bed manufacturers.

(Right) Keeping a bedroom neat should not be a chore for guests. Making up this twin bed is as easy as releasing attached loops of the coverlet from the hooks along the side wall. At night the quilted material hung across the wall creates a cozy enclosure.

(Opposite Page) Guests who like to read before falling asleep will appreciate a basket of books and current magazines. A swing-arm lamp allows guests to pull the light closer for better reading.

Seasonal Change

Twin beds can make a room very flexible and easy to change around. One time of year, you may prefer them parallel to each other, while during another season you can choose to position them at right angles. You can be just as creative and flexible with bedding from season to season.

A spring garden can be a joy any time of year in a room that showcases the vibrant colors and floral cheer of the season. A bright guest room is sure to heighten anyone's spirits. Floral fabrics can be tricky to work with because of the temptation to use them everywhere. Ground the room with a quiet background by covering the walls with a trellis pattern wallpaper. Break up the floral design with a bright, dominant solid color for the duvet or bed cover.

As surely as spring turns to summer and then on to fall, enjoy making seasonal changes to a garden room. Reversible bed coverings, dust ruffles, and window valances make it easy to give a room a whole new look. As the seasons change, florals can turn to plaids and accent colors can be changed by simply turning over bedding and pillows.

ALL THE TRIMMINGS

Details make a difference. In the case of appointing a guest room, they can make all the difference. Tassel trim along the edge of draperies and valances speaks of custom comfort, and embellishments on pillows and bedding can take the look from dull to designer. Don't overlook the fact that pre-made window coverings and soft furnishings can be customized using trims. Not into sewing? If you are discreet, a glue gun works just fine in most cases.

(Above) A curvaceous settee with a flamboyant arm next to a window optimizes daylight reading. Trims on the draperies and pillows and cording on the settee help make this garden room bloom. Many trims can be added to pre-made store-bought window treatments and accessories.

(Opposite Page) In this guest room, the designer found a floral fabric named "Les Saisons" that pays tribute to her client's affinity for changing seasons. The bed cover, dust ruffles, and pillow shams reverse from floral to plaid, depending on the time of year.

Cozy Cottage Style

A small cottage has long been affiliated with comfort, and for good reason. Often bright and cheery, plump and down-filled, a cottage bedroom is a delightful place to visit.

Twin beds are a staple of cottage décor because of their flexibility in smaller rooms. They suit the style, whether they are fitted with white picket fence headboards or a more refined style painted white.

White painted furniture brightens the décor and a combination of florals and simple stripes add to the light-hearted feel. Classic cottage style works well with white mouldings and window coverings that provide optimum sunlight.

A featherbed, while not immediately evident, is a well-appreciated detail once it is time for bed. A few graceful touches such as a scalloped edge on the bedding will make the room a designer's dream.

A few vintage accessories—perhaps a stack of antique valises—give the room a soft, vintage patina. Sepia-tone photographs add to the ambience. If you have time, consider placing photographs in the room of you and your family posing with the person who is visiting.

DEFINING COTTAGE STYLE

Cottage style is probably the easiest decorating scheme to follow because it has such a broad range. It's meant to be a comfortable, lived-in look that often incorporates older furniture and recycled flea-market accessories. Cottage style is mix and match, making it easy to work many of your favorite things into a guest room. Fabrics are plentiful, and florals and stripes happily coexist. If you opt for wood floors over carpeting, choose distressed planks.

The best part of cottage-style decorating is that it allows for a wide interpretation and gives you plenty of room for expressing your own personal style.

(Above) Vintage accessories are a basic component of cottage style. New and old decorative items mix well if new finds have the look of yesteryear.

(Opposite Page) A pretty toile has more impact when it is used for draperies and dust ruffles instead of on every fabric in the room. Simple blue-and-white ticking wallpaper and ecru damask bedspreads, with scalloped edges and blue cording, are perfect choices. The crowning glory of the room is the toile wallpaper border around the top of the walls.

Twin Bed Open Sleigh

Two is better than one when it comes to delightful sleigh beds. While the origin of the sleigh bed is a bit vague, there is no denying they are a decorator's delight. A sleigh bed has a headboard and footboard of the same height, and follows the outlines of a horse-drawn sleigh.

Sleigh bed frames are wonderful canvasses for an artist's brush. When painted with flowers or other whimsical patterns, the beds become a focal point in a guest room.

Sleigh beds offer classic curves and a wide variety of unique styles. You can find sleigh beds made from wood, metal, and a combination of both materials including stylish contemporary metal. They come in a wide range of sizes, including day beds. The curved headboard and footboard design lends to the appeal of these unique beds. Authentic hand carving and a variety of wood finishes all add classic style and charm to the décor of a guest room.

TIPS FOR PAINTING FURNITURE

Painting anything is only as successful as the amount of time invested in gathering the right materials and prepping the project before you start. If you are going for a distressed look, you can be a little more casual about the process of painting furniture. If you are going for a more refined look, be sure to keep these tips in mind:

- Sand surface well
- Use high-quality paintbrush
- Work with oil-based paint (it's more work than water-based paint, but results are more durable)
- Use quality primer
- Sand between coats
- Paint from top to bottom, with grain of wood

(Above) Small details, such as a crystal hung from the bottom point of a valance, add a touch of whimsy to a room.

(Opposite Page) To begin decorating a room, define your inspiration. A pair of hand-painted sleigh beds led to the color palette chosen for this guest room. The attention to detail in other areas of the room, such as the window coverings, honors the beauty of the beds.

Weekends Home

When children leave home for college, they will undoubtedly return accompanied at times by friends. Twin beds make it easy to accommodate their guests. Make weekends and vacation time at home extra special by updating and appointing their former bedroom in the spirit of an opulent suite.

A sophisticated palette of deep burgundy and gold is luxurious and can make family members feel pampered. Details such as professionally framed artwork, quality lamps, and custom bedding will acknowledge your acceptance of their newfound maturity.

Hardworking students who want to sleep in on long-awaited weekends will appreciate blackout honeycomb shades.

(Above) A dramatic color palette, such as burgundy and gold, conveys sophistication and is restful at the same time. The window treatment is both decorative—a valance hung on a 2" mahogany pole with large gold-leaf fleur-de-lis finials—and practical with blackout honeycomb shades.

(Opposite Page) Grown children will be delighted to return home when they know they will be greeted with a luxurious guest room. A comfortable chair and ottoman accompanied by a floor lamp are sure to make a favorite study spot.

Formality with Pizzazz

Formal style is not usually associated with whimsical theme rooms, yet the two can coexist with the right balance of each. Sophisticated antiques and custom bedding join the circus when canopies are hung from monkey brackets, and a scalloped circus tent awning is mounted over drapery panels and Austrian shades.

Look for quality fabrics with subtle prints that convey the theme without overpowering the room's elegance.

FORMAL FABRICS

If you are looking for dressed-up style, consider the following fabrics:

- **Brocade:** A jacquard weave with an embossed effect.
- **Damask:** Usually made from linen, a jacquard weave in a reversible rich pattern.
- **Pima Cotton or Egyptian Cotton:** Excellent quality, comfortable cotton.
- **Polished Cotton:** Satin or plain weave cotton finished to appear shiny.
- **Sateen:** Satin weave cotton fabric.
- **Silk:** A natural protein fiber taken from the cocoon of the silkworm. Available in many weaves, including dupioni, and in many weights. Elegant choice for drapery and bedding.

(Right) An elegant window treatment suggests a circus big top tent and stage curtain and carries through the theme of the room.

(Opposite Page) There's fun under the big top in this guest room appointed with comfortable fabrics.

CHAPTER 6
Double Duty

The reality of most guest rooms is that when there are no guests in the house, the room is likely to do double duty as a home office, craft room, or may serve some other purpose. The trick to making this room welcoming for visitors is to make it clutter-free and well-appointed for their stay.

You don't want to have to throw your world into chaos in preparation for a guest's arrival. A home office is likely to hold important documents, paperwork, and a computer used for business. If you have to fly into a flurry to stash documents and hide piles of paper just before a guest calls, you may spend days trying to locate what you were working on.

Attractive fabric-covered or leather boxes labeled for specific subjects or types of projects can help conveniently switch the use of a room. Consider a bookshelf unit with doors or drawers. Books and decorative accessories can line the shelves, while papers and supplies are quickly—and easily—hidden from view.

(Right) A living area can be modified to become a pleasant place for guests. Design options in sleeper sofas have become very sophisticated, making it impossible to tell that a living room or den does double duty as a guest room.

(Opposite Page) An attractive home office can easily become a guest room if it is well organized. By clearing papers and setting a computer aside, a desk can serve as a dresser top. The desk chair becomes a guest chair and a small office table becomes a bedside table when guests arrive.

Business Experience

Sometimes it takes the experienced eye of an interior designer to see possibilities often overlooked by others. A homeowner needed to use a 12' x 14' room as both a home office and a guest room but could not see how it could be done successfully.

The solution was a wall unit with a rollout desk that accommodates a computer, printer, fax, and files and neatly tucks away at the end of the day. Half the space in the room was designated for a sofa that converts to a bed. A small, attractive wood file cabinet and a fabric-covered round table on either end of the sofa serve as bedside tables when guests visit.

(Above) The desk in an attractive built-in wall unit easily rolls away when overnight guests come to stay. Consider using a small folding screen to hide office equipment.

(Opposite Page) With a well-thought-out plan, a home office can become a gracious guest room. There is no need to sacrifice sleeping comfort with a pullout sofa. Get the best pullout mattress you can afford, with soft padding and firm support.

Double Up

If a home office or craft room is going to serve dual purposes, be sure to make decorating choices that make the room inviting. A room that will welcome guests means disguising the steel filing cabinets—cover them with a colorful throw or vintage tablecloth for a quick camouflage.

Lamps and lighting fixtures should reflect the room's décor and add decorative elements. Look for furniture that is attractive and can serve guests' needs, making their visit comfortable. A bedroom closet may have been removed to accommodate a built-in workspace, so be sure to provide a place to hang clothing and store suitcases.

One of the most important basics in decorating a multi-purpose room is to purchase furniture that does double or triple duty for storage. Purchasing versatile accessories and furniture allows options that give your living space character and flexibility. Consider the following:

- A bed tray can make a collapsible writing desk
- A sleeper-sofa can be a bed for visitors
- Bookcases and armoires, with or without doors, can serve as entertainment centers, home office, or bedroom storage
- Folding chairs with slipcovers make quick, easy seating
- Futons can be a quick fold-out bed
- Lined baskets make attractive portable storage
- Tables with drawers or shelves on their bases offer additional storage
- Wall-mounted lighting saves table space
- Wall shelf units are great for storing towels in the bath

(Right Top and Right) While armoires have moved away from their original purpose of serving as a closet, they still solve many storage challenges.

(Opposite Page) Lamps and light fixtures can add style to a room. Look for lamps with character and decorator style. Lampshades made from interesting materials, such as wicker, and unique shapes add an instant designer look to a room.

Sitting Pretty

A comfortable guest room can also serve as the perfect retreat for activities such as reading or writing when not hosting visitors. A generous chaise lounge—the size of a full bed—paired with a comfortable upholstered chair and ottoman works well. The chaise can be used for relaxation and can easily be dressed for bed by adding sheets, pillows, and blankets.

The transition to a guest room should be easy since a reading and writing room is going to address the same needs as a guest room—a comfortable place to sit, a good chair, a writing area, and good lighting. Both you and your guests will appreciate a gooseneck reading lamp over the top of the chaise lounge.

(Above) Window treatments can be casual without sacrificing style. Simple panels in a salmon and beige print hung from textured iron poles and rings, and accented with matching tassel trim, define elegant style.

(Left) A simple, uncluttered desk is an inviting place to write and will be appreciated by guests who would like to catch up on correspondence or journaling.

(Opposite Page) An extra large chaise provides space to read by day, and a place to sleep at night.

Day Dreaming

A daybed is a classic, and can be a great way to open a room up to other uses when guests are gone. If dressed properly, a daybed can serve as a comfortable sofa. Pillows or bolsters can be used to shorten the depth between a wall and the edge of the bed, making it a relaxing place to sit.

Choose fitted, tailored bed coverings for the daybed to downplay its use as a bed. Be sure that the top cover has slits at the corners so it can accommodate a daybed frame. Otherwise, the coverlet will bunch up and be unsightly.

If a trundle pulls out and pops up, the twin mattresses can be pushed together to make a bigger bed. Foam insert strips can be purchased at a bedding store to fill the gap between the two mattresses.

(Above) A soft shade, framed by a sheer ivory swag, provides privacy and light.

(Left) Attention to detail is what gives a guest room appeal. An ornate iron screen repeats the scroll pattern in the wallpaper, and is echoed on the tapestry fabric used for the large pillows.

(Opposite Page) Daybeds often accommodate a trundle that pulls out to provide an additional twin bed. The advantage is the extra sleeping space; the disadvantage is that the bed frame is so high from the ground that the bed may not make a comfortable sofa during the day. Consider an oversized club chair substitute for day use.

Simple Secrets

If a room is called upon to do double duty, it may hold some secrets. An office desk may fold into an armoire when guests arrive, or a bed may fold out of what looks to be a bookcase at night. Whatever the case, small secrets can make a big difference.

Look for solutions to storage problems such as stackable boxes or an ottoman that opens to hold bedding. If there are no hard surfaces in a small room for a drinking glass or a vase of flowers, use a serving tray on an upholstered stool.

(Above) If hard surfaces in a small guest room are limited, use a serving tray to hold glassware and food items. A tray without sides can make a good writing surface.

(Above Right) Small, stacked decorative cases can serve as a side table and can store paperwork and other items you may want to keep out of sight when guests arrive.

(Opposite Page) Trundle beds are a great space-saving option in a guest room. Look for models with good rolling casters that pull out easily. Since this type of bed does not use a box spring, be discerning when choosing the mattress.

Trundle Up

For small-space rooms, a trundle bed provides additional sleeping space when needed. Instead of a box spring supporting a mattress, the bed is made up of a mattress supported by a frame. Under this structure another bed is housed and can be accessed by simply pulling it out from underneath the main bed. Some of these beds have a mechanism that, when activated, will bring the second bed up to the same height as the main bed.

A quality mattress is especially important with a trundle bed because there is not a box spring to support it. Just be sure that the mattress for the lower bed is not so thick that it will not fit under the frame of the top bed.

Regal Retreat

A personal retreat may have to be shared with guests from time to time. Guests will appreciate the same details that make a room a special hideaway for the host. A creative canopy is a dramatic detail for a retreat and creates a cozy sleeping area for guests.

Large-scale wallpaper patterns, a mix of soft, pleasant colors, and textured furniture such as wicker can create a beautiful, slightly exotic mood. Part of the fun of traveling and visiting new places is enjoying different styles and decorating schemes. Be confident in sharing the way you like to live with guests.

They'll Thank You Notes

LET THE SUN SHINE

There is no substitute for natural light in a room. Often small windows or the room's orientation during sunlight hours keep a room dark. There are several ways to optimize available light, including:

- Hang a mirror on the wall opposite a window to reflect light.
- Choose light colors for paint or wall coverings.
- Don't obstruct light coming through windows with furniture on the inside or outdoor plantings.
- Be sure privacy sheers can be easily moved aside from the window when not necessary.

(Above) A detailed mirror frame brings architectural detail to a room, while a small sculpture, bold wallpaper featuring peacocks, and wicker furniture are a pleasing eclectic blend.

(Opposite Page) A wicker daybed is a comfortable lounging sofa by day and a comfy bed by night. A simple canopy, suspended from a single rod, is a dramatic detail. Mounting a small flagpole in a wall bracket is an easy way to hang a simple canopy as long as the fabric is lightweight.

Triple Duty

At times, space is at a huge premium—a room may need to be an office, an entertainment room, and a place for house guests. The added challenge of the room being an odd shape makes it a true design challenge. Beams and eaves can be turned into cozy nooks and crannies.

If a bed is tucked under an eave, arrange the room so exceptionally tall guests will not hurt themselves when sitting up. The bed may need to be on wheels so it can be easily pulled away from the wall at night. If a desk is placed near a slanted wall, be sure there is access without the chance of bumping heads too.

If a daybed is a sofa by day, you'll want to pass on the higher trundle models. Without the trundle, look for frames with drawers for storing linens. Mixing wood tones and upholstered furniture and choosing pieces with light materials such as wicker will make a room seem spacious and airy.

(Above) Sometimes every inch of an odd-sized room has to be used—and often for more than one purpose.

(Opposite Page) Look for a daybed style that can serve as a comfortable sofa when not in use as a bed. A drawer in the bed frame can provide much-needed storage.

Tropical Vacation

Most people find tropical style to be a relaxing decorating theme. It lends itself well to a room that may be called into use as a guest room. Multi-functional furniture such as a convertible sofa in a palm leaf print and a wicker armoire work well and are in keeping with the tropical theme.

Silk orchid plants and palm trees, along with prints and artwork with tropical themes, enhance the relaxed style. Upholstering one piece of furniture with a palm leaf fabric provides a thematic focal point in the room.

(Above) A secondary entertainment room easily becomes a guest room when necessary. The sofa pulls out into a queen-size bed, while a bistro table and two bar stools serve as a writing area or workspace.

(Opposite Page) Favorite vacation spots often inspire room décor. Tropical artwork purchased on Sanibel Island determined this room's color palette. The window treatment fabric is printed with birds similar to those found in the National Wildlife Refuge on the island.

Grandma's Care

A grandmother has many unspoken rights, and indulging her grand-children is one of them. A grandmother likely feels that the most important visitor in her guest room is a beloved grandchild. When that is the case, the heart takes over and grandma goes out of her way to make the room a warm and inviting playroom by day and fabulous bedroom by night.

Undoubtedly, the floor will be a premium play area, so choose furni-ture that hugs the walls or can be easily moved aside. Daybeds with trun-dles work well in a grandchild's guest room. An armoire or large chest with plenty of storage space will make it easy to stow toys and games out of sight when adults use the room.

YOUTH PROOF

There is no need to forfeit pleasing décor because a room is going to host children. Consider these guidelines for high style without the worries:

- **Ban white:** This just isn't the place for it. Stay away from any light color fabric that can easily become soiled.
- **Fancy is fine:** Don't be afraid of elegant materials just as long as they are durable. Cottons, linen flo-rals, and rich colors can hide stains. Velvets with crushed nap won't show marks. If you stay away from solid fabrics, and go for prints and patterns, it will be easier to disguise spills and stains.
- **Store in style:** Stash toys in attractive baskets, a vintage trunk, or an upholstered storage ottoman.
- **Choose child-friendly furniture:** Paint wood fur-niture. If it scratches or chips it can be easily touched up, or you may want to let it wear in style. Wicker is a good choice because it is light-weight and can be easily wiped clean.

(Above) Gathering baskets can be used to quickly pick up and tuck away children's toys and games after a visit.

(Opposite Page) A grandmother can enjoy the fantasy of a Parisian sidewalk café and feminine frills when decorating a guest room for treasured visits with a granddaughter.

115

CHAPTER 7
Great Guest Baths

When we think of a guest bath in the most ideal terms, we think of a spacious private bathroom. That may not always be possible, and it may require a bit of ingenuity to achieve a special bath area for guests. It is possible to carve out bath privacy in a small space. Many retailers and restoration building catalogs carry small corner sinks and toilets that can be plumbed to fit into tight spots.

If simple plumbing is in place, luxurious details can make a guest's stay a pampering experience. Appointing a bathroom with a scented candle, spa creams and lotions, cotton balls and swabs, and fresh flowers will make guests feel well cared for.

(Right) A small corner fixture makes it possible to fit a sink into a tiny space to give guests privacy by not having to share a bathroom. A scented candle and fresh flowers are pleasant touches.

(Opposite Page) Guests who have traveled by airplane and are likely to have become dehydrated will appreciate a glass and bottled water in the bath area.

117

Privacy, Please

The need for privacy in a bathroom is obvious, yet it often comes at the expense of bright sunlight streaming through a window. There are many alternatives to typical rain glass for privacy. An attractive solution is window film that resembles rice paper. It softly diffuses light and can be applied directly to windowpanes.

We all have a natural tendency to want to see out a window, but no one will notice a view is missing if a window is dressed as a focal point. A dimensional window treatment—such as an awning valance—helps mask the fact that a window is opaque for privacy.

(Above) Glass shelves suspended from hooks by fabric strips with grommets are an interesting place to display collectibles.

(Left) An awning valance in fabric that matches the floral wallpaper gives the bathroom a garden feel. Red beaded tassels add an element of fun and bring out the red accents in the room.

(Opposite Page) Window film resembling rice paper can be applied directly to windows. The film creates privacy without sacrificing sunlight, and its soft diffusing effect makes the bath a cheerful room.

Diversionary Tactics

Nothing motivates redecorating more than knowing guests are on their way. Replacing plumbing fixtures in a bathroom can be very expensive, and often is not an option. An interior designer would suggest that the bath could be redecorated with a connection and a distraction to outdated plumbing fixtures at the same time.

Time may have passed a rose-colored pedestal sink from fashionable to detestable. Selecting a wallpaper border with a hint of rose, installed at sink height, refers back to the fixture, but new lattice wallpaper and a bold Asian theme is a diversionary tactic. Bamboo used to frame the wallpaper border, along with a large faux bamboo framed mirror and other decorative details, are likely to get your guest's attention, averting notice of the fixtures.

Baths built more than 20 years ago likely have outdated color tile. These colors can be turned into classic designs by choosing a contrasting color for walls and using the color of the tile or fixtures as an accent.

UPDATING AN OUTDATED BATH

Completely remodeling a bathroom is a costly and time-consuming undertaking. There are a number of things you can do to freshen up the bath you have:
- Change lighting—banish florescent bulbs
- Change plumbing fixtures
- Install new vanity
- Make custom shower curtain
- Paint walls new color
- Update medicine cabinet with updated style
- Work with colors in old tile to complement, not compete

(Opposite Page) A wallpaper border with a hint of the rose color of the pedestal sink links the fixture to the bathroom's new décor. The lattice-pattern wallpaper and dark framed mirror downplay the sink color and move the eye to the decorative elements of the room.

They'll Thank You Notes

MAKE YOUR OWN BATH SALTS

Guests will feel extra special when their room is stocked with homemade bath salts that can also serve as a great take-home gift. Scent them with your favorite essential oils and choose colors that fit with the room's décor. Or, for a quick alternative, collect pretty soaps, bath gels, and shampoos from your travels and bundle them with a mini package of facial tissue. Don't forget a bit of ribbon!

Materials:
- 1 cup Epsom salts
- 1 cup sea salt
- 2 cups baking soda
- An essential oil of your choice; lavender is relaxing for a bath

Instructions:
1. Combine first three ingredients in large glass bowl. Add 4 teaspoons of essential oil; stir. Store in tightly capped container for at least two days before using.
2. Tint bath salts if you desire by adding 2-3 drops of food coloring into bowl after adding essential oil; stir.
3. To create different colored salts, divide salts equally between two or more large bowls, tint different colors, and carefully pour into clear containers.

Great Cover-Up

An average bathroom can be transformed into a powder room with great ease. Since the tub and shower don't need to be accessed as often as in other baths in the house, the room can be softened with luxurious sheers as a screen. A first sheer can be hung from a rod at ceiling height, straight across the entire tub. A second, more ornate sheer, trimmed with decorative beads or fringe, can complete an elegant look.

The shower can also be easily concealed using a drapery hung from an expandable spring tension rod. Be sure to set the rod in wall brackets so it is secure when a guest needs to push it aside to access the shower.

If the bath has a standard plate glass wall mirror, replace it with a framed decorative mirror to introduce sophistication into the room. Painting ordinary cabinets either a bright white or glossy black, depending on the décor, and adding new drawer pulls will complete a glamorous makeover.

(Above) By replacing a standard wall mirror with a more attractive framed style, a bathroom gets an instant custom look.

(Left) A pair of luxurious sheers screens the tub and shower and softens a guest bath. The more ornate top sheer is draped and held in place with a black feather tieback for a slightly exotic touch.

(Opposite Page) Toile drapery with beautiful trim conceals a glaring white shower and complements the bathroom's faux-painted harlequin walls, countertops, and black-and-white floor.

Faux, You Know

A small guest bath can become an elegant room by using a faux finish on the walls. There are numerous techniques and products available for the do-it-yourself decorator. For those not so inclined, professional faux painters abound. If you want the look of faux-painted walls and prefer to take the easiest route, look to wallpaper.

Once quality wallpaper in a faux-finish pattern is hung, it is nearly impossible to tell that the wall finish is not paint. There are many advantages to wallpaper, including ease and expense. One of the biggest advantages is that you can tape a roll of the paper to the wall and observe the color at different times of the day, in different light, to be sure it is the look you want before it is installed.

HIRING A FAUX FINISHER

Faux finishing is an art and the results are as varied as the artists who specialize in them. Hiring the right finisher for your home requires some research and planning. In order to get the finish you want, you'll want to do your homework.

Visit showcase and model homes to see an assortment of finishes before you decide what you like best. You can also consult local designers to see their work that has been done in other homes.

Get the name and number of the artist that did the finish you like. Be sure to see their actual work rather than small sample boards.

Have the artist visit your home to see the actual job and discuss whether their capabilities fit what you want done.

Get a written estimate from the artist.

Once you have agreed to hire the artist, ask to have a small area of the wall finished so you can be sure it is the look you want.

(Above) A relaxed Roman valance trimmed with antique beaded fringe perfectly complements iridescent faux-finish wallpaper.

(Opposite Page) It is virtually impossible to tell that the faux finish on the walls is wallpaper, and not paint, if a quality paper is chosen and professionally installed.

Seeing Red

Red is a bold hue for a small bathroom and can make a brilliant back-drop for contrasting accents and accessories. Gold is a classic choice to counter red, and the two make a regal pairing. The contrast color is important because it will keep the room from becoming too dark.

A gold-framed mirror and framed artwork break up red walls, keep-ing them from overpowering the room with color. Simple window treat-ments work well with dark walls. Good lighting is a must, so optimize window light and be sure that light fixtures emit bright light.

WORKING WITH DARK PAINT COLORS

Painting walls a dark color can be a challenge if the original wall is white or beige. You'll have the best suc-cess if you apply a primer coat that has been tinted to the dark color you will be using. For instance, if you are planning to take white walls to a deep red, have the primer tinted with red. The walls will look pink after you have applied the primer, but don't despair. After two coats of red paint, they'll be beautiful. Your local paint dealer is the best source for help with tinted primer.

(Right) A red wallcovering is a daring choice for a small bathroom. Gold fabric draped down the corners of the room breaks up the dark color.

(Opposite Page) Decorative accents such as a small wall shelf, framed artwork, or a distinctive mirror softens a bold wall color.

Decorating Drama

A little drama can be a good thing in a guest bath. As long as the theatrics are contained to the decorating scheme, guests will surely enjoy the room. Bold color, stripes, big checks or squares, and texture can make walls exciting. Double crown moulding and painted or papered ceilings can emphasize daring décor.

Grass cloth, burlap, and embossed wallpapers introduce texture and dimension to walls. Be sure that the wallpaper used in a bath can handle moisture.

Tumbled marble, granite, or other natural stone countertops in an interesting color can add to the drama of a guest bath. A furniture-style vanity cabinet is another way to distinguish the look of the room, and is best when crowned with a large, decorative mirror.

WHY WALLPAPER?

Wallpaper has many decorating advantages. When choosing wallpaper for a guest bath, be sure it is made to be hung in a room that is exposed to moisture. Wallpaper can:

- **Add architectural interest:** Wallpapers that look like wood or marble, or have a faux-finish pattern, are an easy way to get a unique look.
- **Create paneling:** Wallpapers and contrasting borders can create decorative wall panels and add architectural interest to flat walls.
- **Hide a bumpy wall:** All-over patterns, extroverted textures and matte wallpaper can minimize bumpy walls.
- **Make a large room more intimate:** Rich, dark, and large-patterned papers bring large rooms down to size.
- **Make a room bigger:** To stretch the look of a room, use small and open patterns in light colors.
- **Raise a low ceiling:** Vertical stripes with an upward thrust make a ceiling look higher.

(Above) Papering the walls of a guest bath in a dramatic dark sage green stripe, topped with a floral border and double crown moulding, and covering the ceiling with a faux marble paper create an elegant room.

(Opposite Page) The choice of woven grass cloth is a case of opposites attracting. The rough, neutral texture of the paper is a good match for the hand-forged wrought iron vanity and mirror.

TRANSFORMING THE ORDINARY

If you are faced with a standard guest bathroom with a builder-grade glass mirror, stark tub and shower area, and awful bright bulb lighting, you are not alone. There are numerous ways you can take a standard bathroom and make it a designer's dream without making radical changes. Here are just a few tricks of the trade:

- Install a lighted makeup mirror with a swing arm on wall near sink.
- Install can lights with soft light bulbs. Put lights on a dimmer. Remove any harsh florescent lighting.
- Install crown moulding and baseboards.
- Paint or paper walls.
- Paint standard wood vanity cabinets a color that suits your scheme.
- Remove plate-glass mirror and replace it with large, attractively framed mirror.
- Treat shower enclosure as large window and install a custom drapery treatment. Be sure there is a liner to protect curtain from water.
- Upgrade faucet and shower fixtures.
- Upgrade towel bars and door hooks.

(Opposite Page) The diamond design wallpaper supplies richness and color to the room and echoes the tile motif in the bathtub. A unique mirror treatment was achieved by upholstering an artist's canvas stretcher frame in faux crocodile fabric, then embellishing it with leather buttons, trims, and tassels. It was then hung from knotted cording and attached over the existing mirror.

(Right) The shower treatment is a shaped cornice covered in chenille that coordinates with the walls and drapery panels in a contrasting light gold. The tailored details and color palette in this guest bath appeals to most tastes.

CHAPTER 8
Creating Comfort

When it comes to welcoming guests, your first priority should be giving them your time and attention. Perhaps you have not seen the glowing face or heard the infectious laughter of this special friend for a very long time. Revel in the closeness and make the most of it.

With this attentiveness comes the knowledge that your friend or family member has traveled far and is tired and perhaps hungry. The comfort of your guests then becomes your next priority, and with a few special touches you can make the visit extraordinary. It doesn't take much to make a stay in your home a memory that will be cherished long after the goodbyes.

You can set the tone for an unforgettable stay the minute you open your front door. As with all successful undertakings, planning is key to being successful. Take your lead from successful innkeepers and know when your guests will arrive. You may be picking them up at a local airport or train station, in which case try to enlist the help of a family member or friend for last-minute details. If guests are arriving on their own, ask for an approximate time of arrival.

Regardless of hour of day, or whether you or someone else is home to prepare, light scented candles and prepare a snack and beverage. Turn on soft music and set out fresh flowers from your garden or a local florist.

If guests are arriving after dark, turn on lights throughout your home. A well-lit house is a cheerful greeting, and will allow you to give guests a graceful orientation tour. If you have excitable pets, consider keeping them closed in another room until you have had a chance to greet guests and make any necessary introductions.

(Above) An extra blanket or comforter should always be available because of the varying preferences in sleeping temperatures.

(Opposite Page) Extra touches such as a new pair of bedroom slippers will surely be appreciated.

133

A Room-by-Room Welcome

While the appointments of a guest room are important, you want guests to feel just as comfortable in other parts of your home. No visitor feels at ease rummaging through drawers or cupboards in search of a drinking glass or piece of silverware. Anticipate their needs by having necessary items in obvious places.

Sitting Room

A guest may be an early riser, and having a light on in early morning hours will encourage them to come into the main living areas of the house. Being able to sit and enjoy the morning paper or a local guidebook is a pleasant way to start the day. If you anticipate guests waking up before you do, consider putting a coffee pot on a timer so a freshly brewed aroma can greet them.

Entry

Some things to consider leaving on an entry table:

- ☐ Daily newspaper
- ☐ Dish of mints
- ☐ Guest book
- ☐ Maps and guidebooks of area
- ☐ Scented candle
- ☐ Soft light left on all night
- ☐ Umbrellas in case of rain

Living Areas

Keeping living areas clutter-free and inviting tells guests they are welcome to enjoy the room. If it contains personal papers spread out over a desk, a guest is not likely to feel it is appropriate to enter. Carefully store paperwork in decorative boxes so it will be easy to return to the task at hand once guests have left.

To make living areas guest friendly, consider:

- ☐ A well-stocked library. Make sure you put out books that you've already read and don't mind your guest taking home
- ☐ Comfortable chairs with good lighting
- ☐ Current magazines, including regional titles
- ☐ Fresh flowers
- ☐ Reading glasses or magnifying glass
- ☐ Soft music and selection of CDs, as well as a note explaining how to work the stereo or music player

(Right) Decorative wall shelves installed in the corner of a room make a good place for a selection of easy reading as well as a spot for decorative accessories.

Dining Room or Kitchen

Before guests arrive, try to have one or two items you know they like and can eat. Your sister's penchant for pistachios or your old roommate's aversion to diet sodas should be remembered. A guest on a special or restricted diet will be very appreciative of familiar foods.

Considerations for eating areas include:

- ☐ Napkins and small plates
- ☐ Non-perishable snacks and fruit set out throughout the day
- ☐ Sugar, sugar substitute, cream, etc. for tea and coffee

Bath

Appointing a bath with luxuries need not be expensive. Customize interesting bottles with attractive labels printed on a computer and fill them with mouthwash, creams, and oils purchased in larger quantities. Let guests know these are gifts to take home as a memory of their visit.

Local shops often carry handmade bath items made from local herbs and plants that will customize the bath and make the visit a unique experience. Following are two lists for the guest bath: one with basics, and one with luxuries rivaling the finest hotels. Both speak volumes of the affection you feel for your guest:

THE BASICS

- ☐ Enough towel rack space
- ☐ Extra tissues
- ☐ Hooks on back of door
- ☐ Lovely bar of milled soap
- ☐ Scented candle
- ☐ Selection of luxury creams and lotions

THE RITZ
(all of the above, plus):

- ☐ Bath salts and oils
- ☐ Bathrobe
- ☐ New razors and shaving amenities
- ☐ New toothbrush and toothpaste
- ☐ Plenty of fresh, plump towels
- ☐ Shelf or counter space for personal items
- ☐ Shower cap
- ☐ Small appliances including hair dryer and curling iron

(Left) Leaving extra toiletries in the bathroom says you are prepared for an overnight visitor. Large, unsightly bottles such as mouthwash can be decanted into smaller bottles with labels customized on a home computer.

(Opposite Page) A kitchen sideboard is the perfect place to lay out a spread of beverages and non-perishable foods. Guests will be especially appreciative if they have traveled from a distant time zone.

Closet

A closet is the perfect place to tuck away items guests may need, but did not have the space to bring with them. If you have the space, hang a clean, comfortable robe for guests to use and include a pair of slip-on slippers.

Other items guests will appreciate include:

☐ Extra blankets and pillows

☐ Hangers, preferably padded, and lots of them. Include pant and skirt hangers

☐ Iron and ironing board

☐ Spare jacket or sweater

☐ Sewing kit

☐ Umbrella

If you are in a resort climate, consider:

☐ Beach towels

☐ Portable folding chair

☐ Sun hat

☐ Sun umbrella

☐ Sunscreen

CLOSET OPTION

If there is not a closet in your guest room, or the one that's there is filled with personal items, an armoire is a good solution. Armoires are versatile and can provide storage for a television as well as hanging space for a guest's clothing. Use drawer space for extra pillows and blankets. Leave at least one drawer empty for guests.

(Right) A simple closet can become a luxurious treat with padded hangers, garment covers, and a coordinating shoe bag. These items are easy to sew and patterns can be found in the home décor section of many pattern books.

Guest Room Tryout

The much-quoted test of a good guest room is to spend the night in the room yourself. While it may seem a bit silly, it is in fact the ultimate comfort test. It is then that you may notice how awkward a lamp is to turn off at night, or you may become aware of the fact that there is nowhere to place a suitcase. So by all means, take your guest room to the test.

Some things to have in the room:

- ☐ Alarm clock (easy to operate), preferably that wakes to music
- ☐ Bedside tables or shelves on either side of bed with plenty of clear space for books, glasses, etc.
- ☐ Current reading material and interesting books
- ☐ Drinking water and non-perishable snacks
- ☐ Flowers—fresh, silk, or paper
- ☐ Framed photo of guest or mutual family and friends
- ☐ High thread count bed linens
- ☐ Luggage rack so guests can easily access the contents of suitcases or carry bags
- ☐ Music player and selection of music
- ☐ One or two comfortable sitting areas
- ☐ Several extra blankets
- ☐ Small welcome gift
- ☐ Soft rugs on either side of guest bed
- ☐ Throw for warding off chills
- ☐ Window coverings for privacy and to control light
- ☐ Writing amenities, including stationery, a nice pen, and stamps

Recreation

If you have a swimming pool or exercise area to share with guests, supply everything they need to use these amenities comfortably.

Guests will also appreciate the following:

- ☐ Maps and suggestions for local nature trails and other outdoor exercise options
- ☐ A reminder to bring workout clothing. Have towels and water bottles handy
- ☐ When you are poolside, show your guest where towels, pool shoes, goggles, and rafts can be found

(Right) Relaxed-style bedding and slipcovers will encourage guests to let go of their routine worries and enjoy their stay.

So Long, Farewell

As with all good things, visits come to an end. If all has gone well, neither you nor your guests will want to say goodbye. Most guests don't want to intrude or make work for their hosts. If guests insist on stripping beds and delivering towels to the laundry, by all means don't argue. They'll feel better, and it will cut down on what needs to be done after their departure.

By accepting any help offered, guests feel comfortable and know they will be welcome into your home again. If there is a drive or flight ahead, pack a light snack for departing guests.

Happy memories will be the souvenir of the visit and you will all enjoy warm and happy thoughts of time spent together in your home.

A FINAL NOTE

The ideas and decorating schemes in this book are meant to inspire, not intimidate. These rooms are in the homes of real people, with everyday lives who have the same constraints you may have when undertaking decorating a guest room. They did work with a design professional, whether you do is a personal decision. Regardless, the designers and homeowners featured shared their ideas with the hope they will give you encouragement to make your guest room a special place.

About the Author

CAROL DONAYRE BUGG

As Vice President and Director of Design to approximately 500 INTERIORS by Decorating Den (IDD) business owners and interior decorators, Carol Donayre Bugg has set out to make the world more beautiful one room at a time. With more than 30 years of experience in design, Bugg has established herself as a credible and knowledgeable designer, businesswoman, author, and lecturer.

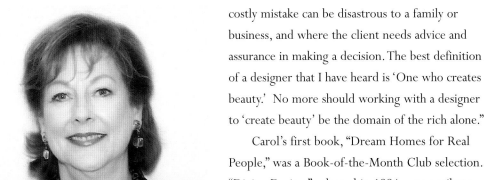

Carol was born in New York City, but has resided most of her adult life in the Washington D.C. area after her father took a diplomatic post at the Peruvian Embassy. She graduated from Georgetown Visitation Jr. College before receiving her formal training at The International Institute of Interior Design in Washington D.C. and the Parsons School of Design in Paris. Carol's design experience includes W & J Sloane in Washington D.C.; The H. Chambers Co. in Baltimore and Washington D.C.; Stix, Baer & Fuller, St. Louis; and the Design Store, Model Home Division, Washington D.C. For 10 years prior to her current affiliation with INTERIORS by Decorating Den she operated Carol Donayre Bugg & Associates, Inc., a successful model home decorating company.

Carol's design history includes projects for the Singapore Embassy, The Congressional Club in Washington D.C., and model home projects for many of the major builders in the D.C. area, including Hillandale in Georgetown. She was the design coordinator for IDD's redecorating of the presidential suite at the Plaza Hotel for Donald Trump, "Life" magazine's American Dream Home, and the "This Old House" showhouse. However, the bulk of her work has revolved around more realistic projects.

The following quote for "The Designer Magazine" exemplifies Carol's philosophy: "So many of my colleagues assume the attitude that a professional designer works only with the affluent client. These designers' budgets for doing a job overwhelm the vast market of middle-income people. A person should be able to hire a decorator who, for a realistic budget, is able to provide the client with beauty, comfort, and good design. Our services are needed more where funds are limited, where a costly mistake can be disastrous to a family or business, and where the client needs advice and assurance in making a decision. The best definition of a designer that I have heard is 'One who creates beauty.' No more should working with a designer to 'create beauty' be the domain of the rich alone."

Carol's first book, "Dream Homes for Real People," was a Book-of-the-Month Club selection. "Divine Design," released in 1994, was a tribute to IDD's 25th anniversary. Carol's third book, "Smart and Simple Decorating," was a Country Homes & Gardens Book Club selection. Ladies' Home Journal, Woman's Day, The Washington Post, and various other publications have featured stories about Carol Donayre Bugg and/or articles written by her. She has been interviewed on the NBC "Today Show," the ABC "Home Show," and "CBS This Morning." Carol has taught design classes for Mount Vernon College and Montgomery Ward, and lectured at the Smithsonian Institution.

Carol has designed several exclusive fabrics. The "First Lady's Tribute" was a patriotic-themed toile inspired by Barbara Bush unveiled at an annual luncheon given by the Congressional wives to honor first ladies. Subsequently, the fabric was presented to Clement Conger, former White House curator, to be used at various State Department functions. Carol also designed "Divine Designs" for a similar luncheon honoring Hillary Clinton. But the fabric closest to Carol's heart is the black-and-white toile named, "Partner's Legacy," she designed to honor the memory of her Labrador retriever. Proceeds from the sale of this fabric benefit Leader Dogs for the Blind.

Carol is a member of the Color Marketing Group (CMG), and has been a member of the American Society of Interior Designers (ASID) since 1974. She is listed in "Who's Who of American Women" and "Who's Who in Interior Design."

On the personal side, Carol is dedicated to her family. Her partner in life and business is her husband of 35 years, Jim Bugg, Sr. She is the stepmother of five children and grandmother of four.

Credits

Index